The Little Tree

Story by Janie Spaht Gill, Ph.D.
Illustrations by Lori Wing

Dominie Press, Inc.

The trees inside the forest grew very thick and high.

Each pushed to be the tallest and grandest in the sky.

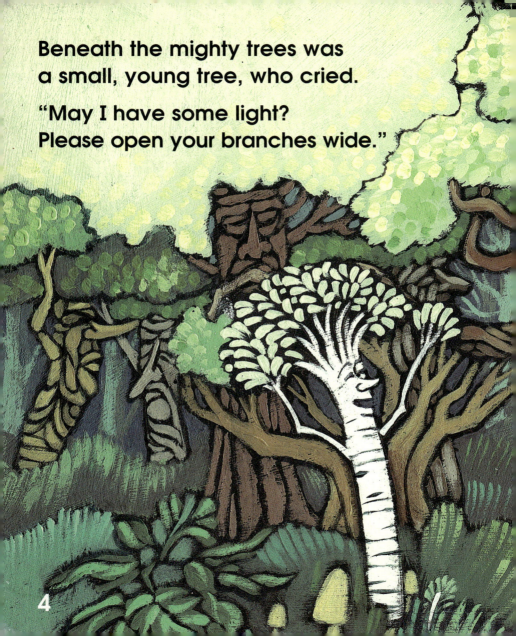

Beneath the mighty trees was a small, young tree, who cried.

"May I have some light? Please open your branches wide."

But the trees were loudly bragging and pushing for more room.

They didn't hear the small tree's voice, who felt that he was doomed.

The trees were all surprised when a storm blew in one day.

Their branches blew and bowed, their heads began to sway.

The wind roared
through the forest,
in sheets the rain poured down.

The trees that once stood
proudly, now bowed their
heads to the ground.

When the storm was over,
the tall trees were cut low.

The small tree stood alone,
who had struggled once to grow.

The little tree cried sadly at the scattered limbs around.

The trees that once bragged loudly were broken to the ground.

The sun's rays bathed his body
in flowing streams from high.

His branches were drawn upward,
toward an opening in the sky.

Beneath his trunk he heard a cry, his eyes then traveled down.

A small, tender tree beneath him had sprouted from the ground.

The little tree remembered
his plight of former days,

so he opened his branches wide
to share the sun's warm rays.

Curriculum Extension Activities

The Little Tree

- Ask the children to write a story about something that is very difficult for them to do or learn. In this story, they should explain what the outcome will be if they keep trying.

- Have the children note the daily weather on a calendar. They can write *cold, sunny, windy, rainy,* etc., or they can draw a small picture depicting the weather on a given day.

- Discuss with the children the four seasons and how the seasons cause changes in flowers and the leaves on the trees. Divide a paper into fourths and have the children draw and label a tree in each of the four seasons.

About the Author

Dr. Janie Spaht Gill brings twenty-five years of teaching experience to her books for young children. During her career thus far, she has taught at every grade level, from kindergarten through college. Gill has a Ph.D. in reading education, with a minor in creative writing. She is currently residing in Lafayette, Louisiana with her husband, Richard. Her fresh, humorous topics are inspired by the things her students say in the classroom. Gill was voted the 1999-2000 Louisiana Elementary Teacher of the Year for her outstanding work in primary education.

Publisher: Raymond Yuen
Editorial Consultant: Adria F. Klein
Editor: Bob Rowland
Designer: Natalie Chupil
Illustrator: Lori Wing

Copyright © 2003 Dominie Press, Inc. All rights reserved. No part of this publication may be reproduced or transmitted in any form or by any means without permission in writing from the publisher. Reproduction of any part of this book, through photocopy, recording, or any electronic or mechanical retrieval system, without the written permission of the publisher, is an infringement of the copyright law.

Published by:

Dominie Press, Inc.
1949 Kellogg Avenue
Carlsbad, California 92008 USA

www.dominie.com
(800) 232-4570

Softcover Edition ISBN 0-7685-2179-3
Library Bound Edition ISBN 0-7685-2487-3

Printed in Singapore by PH Productions Pte Ltd
1 2 3 4 5 6   PH   05 04 03

Dominie Level	Guided Reading	DeFord Assessment
20	L, M	9